Happiness

ADULT COLOURING

Happiness can be found in the smallest things and much closer to home than you think. A few crayons or pencils, this colouring book and a little time – that is all you need.

Browse through the book and choose an illustration that appeals to you. Just start colouring and don't think too much: there is no wrong way of doing it. Experience how wonderfully relaxing colouring is and colour yourself happy! You can keep the illustrations for yourself or use them as presents. You probably have a great spot in your home for the large poster, or colour it in and make someone else happy. This book promises hours of colouring fun and relaxation.

Made by :

....

For :

....

Made by:

....

For:

....

Made by:

....

For:

....

Made by :

....

For :

....

Made by :

....

For :

....

Made by :

....

For :

....

Made by :

....

For :

....

Made by :

For :

Made by :

....

For :

....

Made by :

....

For :

....

Made by:

....

For:

....

Made by :

....

For :

....

Made by :

For :

Made by :

For :

Made by :

....

For :

....

Made by :

For :

Made by :

....

For :

....

Made by :

For :

Made by :

....

For :

....

Made by :

....

For :

....

Made by :

....

For :

....

Made by :

....

For :

....

Made by :

....

For :

....

Made by :

....

For :

....

Made by :

For :

Made by :

For :

Made by :

For :

Made by :

....

For :

....

Made by :

....

For :

....

Made by :

....

For :

....

Made by :

....

For :

....

Made by :

....

For :

....

Made by:

....

For:

....

Made by :

For :

Made by :

....

For :

....

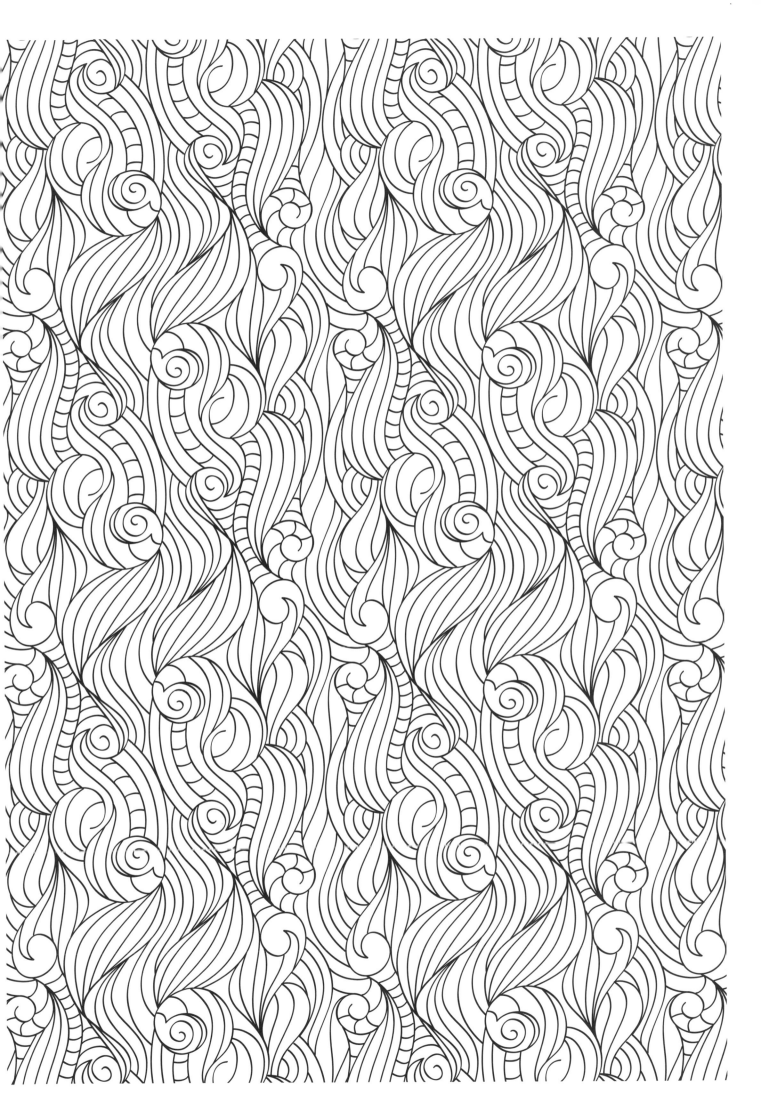

Made by :

....

For :

....

Made by :

....

For :

....

Made by :

....

For :

....